SHEERNESS
NAVAL DOCKYARD
& GARRISON

The Muster Bell Post inside the South Gate, for many years a familiar sight to employees as they entered and left the dockyard.

SHEERNESS
NAVAL DOCKYARD
& GARRISON

David T. Hughes

TEMPUS

Sheerness Dockyard and the garrison beyond.

First published 2002
Reprinted 2003

Tempus Publishing Limited
The Mill, Brimscombe Port,
Stroud, Gloucestershire, GL5 2QG
www.tempus-publishing.com

British Library Cataloguing in Publication Data.
A catalogue record for this book is available from the British Library.

ISBN 0 7524 2762 8

Typesetting and origination by Tempus Publishing Limited
Printed in Great Britain by Midway Colour Print, Wiltshire

Contents

Acknowledgements

I would like to express my indebtedness to the following organisations and institutions for their valuable assistance during my researches for this book, both by providing help when required, and by allowing me to reproduce photographs and other material held in their collections and/or for which they held the copyright: the Ministry of Defence (for permission to use photographic material of unidentified provenance that might be deserving of the attribution 'Crown Copyright/MOD. Reproduced with permission of the Controller of Her Majesty's Stationary Office'); the Chatham Dockyard Historical Society; the Maidstone Museum and Bentlif Art Gallery; the Royal Engineers' Library; and the Sheppey Local History Society. I must also give thanks to the several individuals who generously gave time and help, particular mention going to Fred Buddle, Peter Goss, Giles Guthrie and Brian Sinclair.

Introduction

The Isle of Sheppey, some nine miles long and half as wide, lies on the southern side of the Thames estuary and is separated from the north Kent coast by a narrow channel of the sea called the Swale. Sheerness in the mid-seventeenth century was a short, beak-shaped point of uninhabited marshland jutting out of the north-western tip of the island. To mariners it was generally referred to as the Ness or the Point.

Inhospitable though the place was, there were those who were beginning to recognise its strategic potential. Between Sheerness and the opposite Isle of Grain lay the mouth of the River Medway and up river at Chatham was the fleet anchorage of the Royal Navy. Those who controlled Sheerness thus held the key to the river and had the fate of England's warships in their hands.

Sheerness was also becoming of interest to the Admiralty for another reason. The three royal naval dockyards of the Thames and Medway – Deptford, Woolwich and Chatham – were all sited up river at some distance from the sea. Ships using these yards for minor repairs and maintenance found the passage up river to be a rather tedious exercise which, for a large sailing ship relying on favourable winds and tides, might require days rather than hours. A similar problem existed for ships at the yards when they were ordered to put to sea. They had to first negotiate the river before being able to enter the widening and deepening waters of the Thames estuary.

A short distance off Sheerness lay the Nore, a long east-west sandbank producing a large stretch of calmer water used by the navy as a convenient anchorage. Ships anchoring at the Nore, in need of small repairs of the kind necessitated through the normal wear and tear of ships at sea, would, rather than having to go up to one of the dockyards, carry out the work themselves; the crews used materials that were shipped down to them, occasionally employing shipwrights if more specialised tasks were involved. Re-victualling was also carried out off Sheerness, supplies being brought from Chatham, or from Queenborough, the little Sheppey borough that stood on the banks of the Swale about two miles to the south of Sheerness Point. Likewise fresh powder and shot for the ordnance would be conveyed down river to the waiting ships.

When a war with the Dutch began in March 1665, the two enemies faced each other across the North Sea, which was thus likely to be the major arena for any naval engagements. Geography dictated that it would fall mainly to the dockyards of the Thames and Medway to maintain the ships of the English fleet in a battle-ready condition. Minds began to concentrate at the Admiralty on ways to overcome the problems presented by these dockyards in regard to the wartime need for a quick turn-round of ships coming in for new stores and repairs.

What was required was a new facility having immediate access to the open sea and located where it could work in conjunction with the river yards. For this purpose the Isle of Grain was considered as was Queenborough. Also contemplated was Sheerness which was already put to some use by the navy, the broad mudflats exposed at low tide off the foreshore on the southern side of the Point having for some years been utilized for the careening of ships – examining, cleaning and effecting minor repairs on the normally submerged parts of their hulls. In the end it would be Sheerness that would find most favour as being suitable for the required purpose.

While the size and form of a new yard at Sheerness was still being pondered, the needs of the ships at the Nore were in need of more immediate attention and, in the spring of 1665, a small ready-to-use victualling storehouse was erected adjacent to the foreshore near the Point. As readily available supplies of spare masts, yards, rigging and canvas came into demand to keep the fighting ships at sea, a stockpile of these stores was also begun at Sheerness in what was rapidly turning into a ramshackle little depot.

In August a party of senior naval officials, including the great Samuel Pepys, landed at Sheerness to survey the ground and peg out the proposed layout for the new dockyard. Events then started to move quickly. The work of construction was shortly put in hand and, by mid-November, had been sufficiently advanced for it to be announced that thenceforth the large ships of the navy would be refitted there. In the meanwhile, adjacent to the dockyard at the Point, work on erecting a fort to contain twenty-nine pieces of ordnance was also underway. In comparison with the need-driven rate of construction for the dockyard, however, progress on the fort would prove painfully slow.

The fort was still not completed when, in June 1667, a Dutch fleet appeared over the horizon intent on attacking the fleet in the Medway in precisely the way that the fort was being constructed to prevent. The fort, under-manned and with most of its armaments not yet in place, had only seven guns which could be made immediately serviceable. After an exchange of fire with the encroaching enemy ships, the defenders decided to give up the unequal struggle, and hurriedly abandoned the fort to its fate. The Dutch, landing shortly afterwards, were thus able to march into both fort and dockyard without opposition. With Sheerness in their hands the Dutch ships began the next phase of their operation. Advancing up the River Medway, they decimated the ships of the English fleet that they found moored there. The triumphant Dutch then sailed back to Holland, but not before they had destroyed the fort and laid waste the dockyard at Sheerness. A few weeks later a peace treaty was concluded with the English.

The capture of the fort and dockyard, and subsequent wrecking of the fleet had been a massive blow to English pride. To prevent repetition of the disaster, plans were immediately drawn up and put into effect to build a far more powerful fortress at Sheerness. At the same time action was initiated at the dockyard to get it back into an operational condition as quickly as possible. By the end of 1672 work on the sturdy fort and adjacent dockyard had both reached completion. Thus there came to be established at Sheerness an association with the navy and military that was destined to endure for the next three centuries.

One

The First Dockyard and Fort

Sheerness, unlike the other English dockyards, had no substantial town nearby and, for many years, the workmen had to be accommodated in hulks, or old ships, which had been sunk on the muddy foreshore in front of the dockyard to act as breakwaters. Spartan living conditions would long prevail for the hulk dwellers at Sheerness where the necessities of life remained scarce, even fresh water having to be shipped in. In the huge areas of marshland on the landward side of Sheerness, the ague – a form of malaria – prospered, and few who spent any time at Sheerness would be spared from its ravages. As the old hulks decayed they, and the area behind them, were infilled with earth, thus creating new ground for the dockyard, and new hulks were sunk in front of them. In addition to the hulk-borne community a small shanty town, known as Blue Town, later began to develop beyond the southern boundary of the dockyard, so called, it was said, from the colour of the paint that had been purloined from the dockyard to paint the buildings. In the latter half of the eighteenth century a new outlying colony, Mile Town (a mile from the dockyard), also began to spring up, forming the nucleus of the modern town of Sheerness.

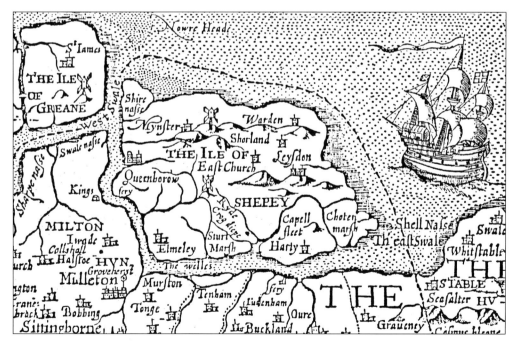

A map of Sheppey in the earlier part of the seventeenth century when Sheerness, at the north-western tip of the island, was merely an uninhabited marsh.

HET EYLAND

SCAPEIA of QUINENBURG.

Sheerness Fort captured and being ransacked by the Dutch in July 1667, a precursor to a further catastrophe with the destruction of the English fleet in the Medway.

The fort, in the latter part of the seventeenth century, having been rebuilt in a substantially strengthened form following its humiliating fall to the Dutch.

Generations of dockyard families were born, lived and died on the old hulks at Sheerness such as those shown here in 1740.

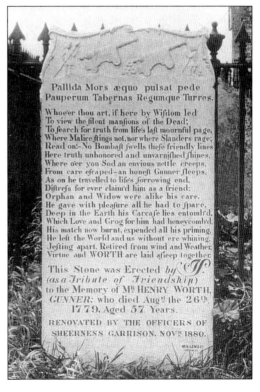

Pallida Mors æquo pulsat pede
Pauperum Tabernas Regumque Turres.

Whoe'er thou art, if here by Wisdom led
To view the silent mansions of the Dead;
To search for truth from life's last mournful page,
Where Malice stings not, nor where Slanders rage;
Read on:-No Bombast swells these friendly lines
Here truth unhonored and unvarnished shines,
Where o'er yon Sod an envious nettle creeps,
From care escaped–an honest Gunner sleeps.
As on he travelled to life's sorrowing end,
Distress for ever claim'd him as a friend;
Orphan and Widow were alike his care,
He gave with pleasure all he had to spare,
Deep in the Earth his Carcase lies entomb'd,
Which Love and Grog for him had honeycomb'd,
His match now burnt, expended all his priming,
He left the World and us without ere whining,
Jesting apart, Retired from wind and Weather,
Virtue and WORTH are laid asleep together.

This Stone was Erected by
(as a Tribute of Friendship)
to the Memory of Mr HENRY WORTH,
GUNNER; who died Augt the 26th
1779, Aged 57 Years.
RENOVATED BY THE OFFICERS OF
SHEERNESS GARRISON. NOV^r 1880.

In addition to the fort, protection of Sheerness from attack was provided by a guardship stationed off the Point. In 1775 the *Conquestador* (sixty guns) was allocated to the duty. The gravestone of her gunner, Henry Worth, who was buried in Minster churchyard on 31 August 1779, carried an interesting inscription.

A group of ships 'in Ordinary' (laid up out of commission) near the Point at Sheerness in a westward-looking view from 1793.

Ships in a squall at the Nore, the fleet anchorage off Sheerness; the fort and dockyard are shown on the horizon to the left-hand side of the picture. In 1797 a great mutiny broke out among the crews of the fleet stationed at the Nore against the harsh and often unjust conditions under which they served.

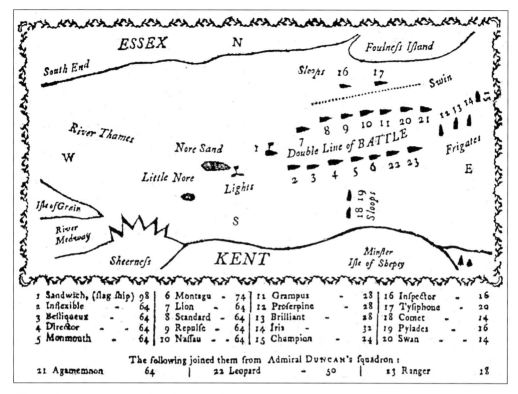

ESSEX   N

South End   Foulness Island

Sloops 16   17   Swin

River Thames   8 9 10 11 20 21   12 13 14

W   Nore Sand   7   Double Line of BATTLE   Frigates

Little Nore   2 3 4 5 6 22 23   E

Lights

Isle of Grain   18 19 Sloops

River Medway   S

Sheerness   KENT   Minster
Isle of Shepey

1	Sandwich, (flag ship)	98	6	Montagu	74	11	Grampus	28	16	Inspector	16
2	Inflexible	64	7	Lion	64	12	Proserpine	28	17	Tysiphone	20
3	Belliqueux	64	8	Standard	64	13	Brilliant	28	18	Comet	14
4	Director	64	9	Repulse	64	14	Iris	32	19	Pylades	16
5	Monmouth	64	10	Nassau	64	15	Champion	24	20	Swan	14

The following joined them from Admiral DUNCAN's squadron :

| 21 | Agamemnon | 64 | 22 | Leopard | 50 | 23 | Ranger | 28 |

Above: A contemporary plan showing the disposition and names of the ships implicated in the mutiny at the Nore.

Right: On board the *Sandwich*, Dick Parker, the leader of the mutineers, presented Admiral Charles Buckner, commander-in-chief at the Nore, with a list of the seamen's demands.

13

Left: As days went by with negotiations stalemated, the men lost heart, and the mutiny collapsed. The ringleaders were arrested, those most involved being sentenced to death. At his execution on board the *Sandwich*, Parker was given a glass of wine before being hanged from the yardarm.

Below: The northern aspect of the dockyard and fort in 1810. By this time the final decisions were being made in regard to a total rebuilding of the dockyard.

Two
The Great Rebuilding

The presence of the old hulks gave a stability to the reclaimed land being used in the dockyard but, as their carcasses began to rot (as did the wooden wharf walls behind which they lay), there was a growing danger of large sections of the dockyard falling back into the sea. By the first years of the nineteenth century the situation had become so serious that drastic action was required, and, in 1813, a major rebuilding of the dockyard was got underway. The scheme adopted for the reconstruction was that of the noted civil engineer, John Rennie. More reclaimed land was to be used, being protected from the sea behind a massive granite outer wall. The difficulties of construction on soft foundations of mud were tremendous and extensive deep piling was used for all the major structures. The first phase of the work – the Great Basin with its three dry docks and associated buildings – was formally opened on 5 September 1823 by Admiral of the Fleet, the Duke of Clarence, third son of George III. The Small Basin and Boat Basin were the next to be finished, the erection of the various necessary workshops, accommodation and other buildings continuing for several more years before the new dockyard, occupying sixty acres, was finally complete.

Works in hand near the Point for the major rebuilding of the dockyard. In the background on the right can be seen buildings within the old fort.

A southwards view of the sea wall under construction with, in the centre, the new-built Officers' offices and, behind them, the five-storey victualling storehouse.

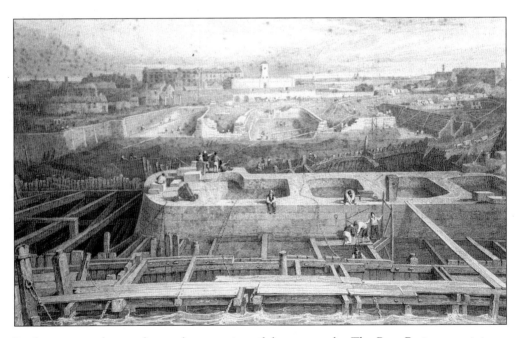

Looking eastwards over the northern portion of the new works. The Boat Basin, containing a slipway and two dry docks, is seen in a well advanced stage of construction.

The completed Great Basin viewed across its cassioned entrance from the sea. The cassion was basically a large wooden container that was floated into position and flooded so that it sank down locating grooves in the walls of the entrance and sealed the basin, thus making it non-tidal.

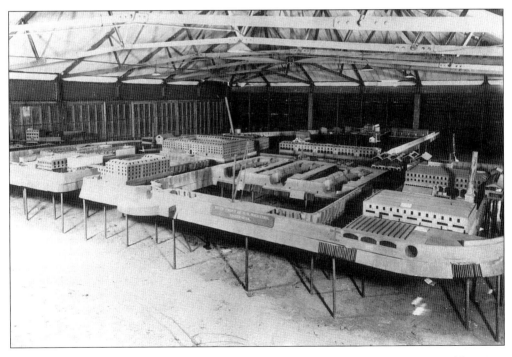

The dockyard model, contemporary with the rebuilding of the yard, was constructed by Navy Board modellers under the supervision of James Mitchell. It took seven years to complete and cost £1,500. Built to a scale of 1in representing 5ft, the model was 40ft long and 36ft at its greatest width.

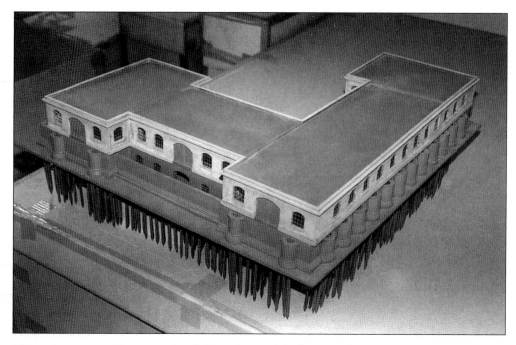

The ordnance store house, a detail from the model, showing the extensive foundations and piling that the new dockyard buildings required due to the unstable nature of the ground.

Admiralty House, erected during 1827. In the spring of that year the Duke of Clarence had been created Lord High Admiral, and it was anticipated that Admiralty House would become his official residence.

In June 1830 George IV died, bringing Clarence, his eldest surviving brother, to the throne as William IV. Clarence's Coat of Arms, made to be installed over the portico of Admiralty House but not used, was carefully preserved and today has a safe home in the museum at Chatham Historic Dockyard.

An early photographic view of Admiralty House which became the residence of the commander-in-chief at the Nore, a role which it retained until the Command Headquarters was moved to Chatham at the beginning of 1907.

UNRIVALLED ATTRACTION!!

PRIVATE THEATRE,
Admiralty House,
SHEERNESS.

On MONDAY, DECEMBER 5th, 1836,

Will be Presented (for the first time on these boards,)

A HANDSOME HUSBAND.

Mr. Wyndham....................CAPTAIN HENRY SMITH, R. N.
Henry Fitzherbert..............THE HON. R. FULKE GREVILLE,
Stephen ....JAMES E. KATON, ESQ. R. N.

Mrs. Wyndham ....MISS ELPHINSTONE FLEEMING.
The Hon. Mrs. Melford.........MISS RAIMBACH.
Mrs. Twysden ....MRS. WM. T. SMYTH.

To conclude with the popular Farce of

Perfection;
OR, THE LADY OF MUNSTER.

Sir Laurence Paragon...........LIEUTENANT CARR, R. M.
Charles Paragon ....THE HON. R. FULKE GREVILLE.
Sam ....CAPT. HENRY SMITH, R.N.

Susan........................MRS. WM. T. SMYTH.
Kate O'Brien ....MISS ELPHINSTONE FLEEMING,

IN WHICH CHARACTER SHE WILL SING

" I'll be no submissive Wife," and "La mia crudel Tiranna."

VIVANT REX ET REGINA.

W. KNEWSTUB, PRINTER AND BOOKBINDER, SHEERNESS.

Handbill from 1836 announcing a function at Admiralty House. The building became the venue for various soirées and social occasions to which the naval, dockyard and military officers, along with favoured prominent townspeople, were invited.

Admiralty House seen from the gardens at the rear of the building in another early photograph.

The waterfront at Blue Town, Sheerness, in 1830, looking northwards towards the dockyard. The Fountain Inn, seen in the centre of the picture, provided convenient accommodation for officials visiting the yard.

The landing place at Blue Town, Sheerness, in 1830, with the dockyard on the right. Sheerness was at the time in great want of a pier that could be used by larger merchant vessels. The space between the landing place and the dockyard was known as Rats Bay.

The Boat Basin of the new yard looking southward in 1830, with some construction work still going on in the foreground.

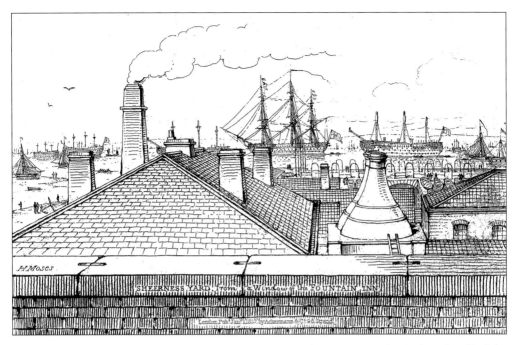

A peep from an upper window of the Fountain Inn gave this view over the dockyard wall of the southern section of the newly built dockyard.

Another view across the dockyard from the upper windows of the Fountain Inn looks in a north-westerly direction past the steam engine house towards the Great Basin.

The *Trafalgar* (106 guns), which had been launched in 1820 at Chatham Dockyard after seven years on the stocks, seen tied up on the western side of the Great Basin at Sheerness. Early in 1825 her name was changed to *Camperdown*.

A frigate under repair in the Great Basin, her sails, rigging and guns taken out, and all masts and spars removed except the lower masts.

Hulks in harbour off the dockyard wall at Sheerness. Since 1802 such vessels were no longer used to house the families of the dockyard men.

By 1832 the finishing-off work on the new yard had been completed, with the Royal Navy having at its disposal a compact and efficient new facility which would be well utilised for the maintenance of its fighting ships.

Looking eastwards towards Sheerness from the sea with the dockyard on the left. On the right is the new town pier which was officially opened by Admiral Charles E. Fleeming, commander-in-chief at the Nore, on 8 September 1835.

Busy harbour scene at Sheerness. The years following the rebuilding of the dockyard would be a golden age for both the yard and town. The dockyard would enter a phase of the greatest activity it would ever know, while the town, finding a new confidence, began a sustained period of improvement and expansion.

Three
Victoria's Dockyard

When Queen Victoria commenced her long reign in 1837, there stood at Sheerness a state-of-the-art dockyard for the building and repair of the great oak-built and broadside-firing sailing ships of the Royal Navy which, by the time of Trafalgar, were reaching the peak of their perfection. But this was in an age when Britain, with momentum provided by the Industrial Revolution, was undergoing an accelerating pace of technological advance, with radical changes in naval architecture following in its wake. Even as the new dockyard was being formally opened in 1823, the seeds of its obsolescence were being planted. At Deptford in the previous year the navy launched its first steam-driven fighting vessel, the Comet, *of 238 tons. As the nineteenth century progressed, the yard would have to continuously update its facilities and skills to meet the ever shifting demands of warship design: sail gave way to steam, paddle to propeller, and wood to iron then steel. These and many other changes were reflected in the new roles being allocated to traditional dockyard buildings, were the working mast house, which were being converted for engineering use as machine and fitting shops.*

The launch of the *Rattler* from the slip on 13 April 1843. Laid down in April 1942 as a wooden paddle-sloop, she was converted to a screw-propeller ship whilst under construction and was subsequently used for a successful series of propeller evaluation trials.

A trial took place off Sheerness on 3 April 1845 in order to compare propeller with paddle propulsion. The *Rattler* was tied stern to stern with the *Alecto*, a paddle vessel of similar size and engine power, for a tug of war. The *Alecto* was pulled astern at 2.8 knots.

The *Camperdown* (formerly the *Trafalgar*, renamed in February 1825) was moored in harbour at Sheerness in the summer of 1843 as the flagship of Admiral Sir Edward Brace, commander-in-chief at the Nore.

On 12 July 1843 the *Camperdown* had a number of civilian guests on board. When a ship bearing Leopold, King of the Belgians, sailed by, the *Camperdown* fired a royal salute causing one of the portable magazines to accidentally blow up. The daughter and niece of the Vicar of Eastchurch were among those who died in the explosion.

The Sheerness Royal Dockyard Brigade making a mock attack on Queenborough in August 1852. In 1847 the Admiralty had formed the men of the yard into this local protection force, commanded by their dockyard officers. They were paid 6*d* an hour and exercised after working hours. At the end of recruitment there were 890 men. They were disbanded in 1857.

The hulk *Devonshire* (seventy-four guns) moored at Sheerness after being put into harbour service in 1849. The Crimean War having begun in 1853, she was ordered to be prepared as a receiving ship for Russian prisoners of war in mid-August of the following year.

Russian prisoners of war between decks on the *Devonshire* after being put on board at the beginning of September 1854. Over a thousand Russian soldiers, many accompanied by their wives and children, were accommodated in the hulk.

A very early photograph of shipwrights at Sheerness Dockyard posing in the frames of a new ship under construction on the slipway in the Boat Basin.

A steam factory for the repair and fitting of ships' propulsion machinery was established at Sheerness in 1854. This photograph, dating from around 1859, shows its interior. In September 1861 a new entrance, known as Factory Gate (afterwards South Gate), was made in the dockyard wall for the convenience of the men employed in the factory.

The *Collingwood* (eighty guns) in No.2 Dry Dock across the Great Basin. She was undocked in July 1861 having been fitted with an engine and propeller. The stern of the *Seven* is on the right.

The brig-sloop gunvessel *Griffon* (five guns) in No.4 Dry Dock where she had been placed in June 1860 for a survey. Returning in 1865 from a gruelling three years of patrolling the west coast of Africa, she was brought back into the dockyard for an extensive refit.

From 30 December 1860 security of the dockyard had been placed in the hands of the Metropolitan Police (Dockyard Division). A group of the policemen are shown, dressed in their uniform of navy blue swallow-tail coats and stove pipe hats. In 1865 the hats were replaced by a combed police helmet.

A dockyard policeman standing at the northern end of Dockyard Terrace, an elegant row of five houses built in 1828 to accommodate the principal officers of the yard.

The *Duncan* (101 guns) flagship at Sheerness in March 1874. Superficially looking like the kind of ship with which Nelson would have been familiar, the *Duncan* was another of the vessels of the changing navy to have been fitted with an engine and propeller in addition to her sails.

The cruiser *Diamond*, launched from the slip at Sheerness on 26 September 1874. She was the last purely wooden ship to be built by the dockyard. An interesting example of the transitional phase of naval architecture from sail to steam; when fully rigged she could sail as fast as when using her propeller and engines – around thirteen knots.

The sloop *Gannet*, launched from the slip at Sheerness on 31 August 1878, was one of the dockyard's earliest ships with a composite construction of iron and timber.

The *Gannet* undergoing restoration at Chatham in 2001. She is the sole survivor of well over a hundred warships built at Sheerness during the life of the dockyard.

The dockyard school, erected in 1892 on the site of the old plank shed. In 1842 it had been ordered that a school for apprentices should be set up. The original classroom was in one of the storehouses, the dockyard having to wait half a century for a custom-built school building. In 1952 the name was changed to Dockyard Technical College.

Dockyard apprentices from the 1894 entry at the time of their coming out in 1900, after their six years' apprenticeship. Many apprentices of humble background rose through the dockyard schools to achieve high positions in the Admiralty.

Four

The Garrison

During the rebuilding of the dockyard, land formerly occupied by the southern section of the fort had been taken in, and the military establishment became relocated along a coastal strip that stretched eastwards, from what was now being called Garrison Point, between the foreshore and the northern boundary of the dockyard. Within this area a new parade ground, barrack blocks and other needed buildings were established. Along the top of the beach a long raised line of gun emplacements, musketry walls and other defences was erected facing the sea. Into these defences was later inserted the centre bastion, a powerful gun battery completed in 1850. To catch any enemy ships trying to enter the harbour in a crossfire, in 1855 a Martello-style tower was erected on the Isle of Grain opposite Garrison Point. At Garrison Point a new fort, thirteen years in the building, was completed early in 1877. More compact but much stronger than its predecessor, it was robustly constructed out of Cornish granite, could accommodate a garrison of 360 men, and contained some impressive heavy ordnance with which to command the entrances to the Thames and Medway.

A photograph, dating from 1859, showing a group of army personnel stationed in Sheerness Garrison.

The Tipperary militia on parade in the Garrison, 5 July 1860, ready for an inspection by Major General Bloomfield, Inspector General of Artillery. No music was played or guns fired on the occasion out of respect for Captain Ruddle B. Watson, Dockyard Superintendent, who had died that morning.

Garrison Point Fort while under construction. A view from the foreshore while the heavy wrought iron plating to protect the gun embrasures was being installed.

The southern flank of Garrison Point Fort during the installation of the protective iron shielding which took eighteen months to complete; in all nearly 2,000 tons of $4\frac{1}{2}$ in thick armoured plate was used.

The interior of the fort as construction neared completion. It was formally handed over to the Royal Artillery by the contractors, Henry Lee & Sons, on 31 January 1877.

The new fort at Garrison Point. It was shaped like a capital letter D, with its main armaments facing seawards on its curved side and situated in galleries on two tiers, each of which carried nineteen guns.

An officer and his lady with one of the heavy guns in Garrison Point Fort. The guns, which weighed twelve tons each, were muzzle-loaded and heavily rifled. They were capable of firing a 9in 250lb shell with a maximum range of about three miles and penetrating the armour of an iron-clad warship at 1,000 yards.

View from Garrison Point Fort looking eastwards, with part of the Albemarle gun battery in the right-hand corner. The bathing machine on the beach was reserved for the exclusive use of the family of the commander-in-chief at the Nore.

An artilleryman posing by one of the sixty-four-pounder muzzle-loading guns on the garrison's gun batteries. Ready-use ammunition is in the foreground.

Range of houses, adjacent to Admiralty House, built as married quarters for the officers of the garrison.

The officers' quarters, erected next to the parade ground and facing the dockyard wall.

The main road into Blue Town with the entrance to the garrison on the right.

The barrier guard house at the entrance to Sheerness Garrison.

The entrance to Well Marsh, standing on the opposite side of the road to the entrance to the garrison. The military hospital stood on the left, about 200 yards inside the entrance.

Naval Terrace and the church, viewed from the guard house, with various army personnel posing in the foreground.

The dockyard church, built in yellow brick and sandstone with its entrance, through a grand portico of Ionic free-standing columns supporting stone pediments, at the eastern end.

Interior of the church, looking westwards towards the altar, showing the gallery and Venetian west window.

View across the Boat Basin towards the harbour, with the garrison's gun wharf and the guns of the saluting battery on the right-hand side.

Looking along the gun wharf with the dockyard's covered slipway and boat houses in the background, and one of the dockyard paddle-tugs alongside the wall.

46

Five
The Gunnery School

The Royal Naval Gunnery School was established on 24 April 1892 in the building, positioned between the entrances of the Great and Small Basins, built in 1821 as a victualling storehouse, but in use as a naval barracks since 1854. The sum of £9,000 was allocated to the founding of the school. Some interior alterations were carried out to the building, drill sheds were erected at the naval recreation ground and also along the coast at Barton's Point, where a gun shed and magazines were constructed for a battery of nine-pounder guns, and a rifle range set up for use by the school. Within a few years of opening, the Gunnery School had outgrown its accommodation. In 1898 the Admiralty proposed to erect new buildings, capable of housing thirty officers and 1,000 men, but the plan was dropped when the only available site proved unsuitable. Eventually it was decided to relocate gunnery and field training at Chatham and, on 26 June 1908, the final parade of the school took place at Sheerness; at its conclusion the Gunnery School band played Auld Lang Syne. *At the end of the month the school vacated its building, which from 1 July became an accommodation depot, its west wing used as offices for the staff of the Home Fleet.*

The Royal Naval Gunnery School situated to the south of the entrance to the Small Basin in the former victualling storehouse.

The covered quadrangle of the Gunnery School, the uses for which included a drill hall, gymnasium and a venue for the social functions organised by the school.

Sailors in the quadrangle awaiting an official inspection of their kit.

A Gunnery School instructor giving quick-firing gun drill; two dockyard policemen look on.

Another quick-firing class in progress. In the background, on the other side of the entrance to the Small Basin, can be seen the offices of the naval officers.

A maxim gun class taking place in the covered quadrangle of the Gunnery School.

Training for shore work on rough ground, a maxim gun being carried on poles. Sheerness-trained naval gunners would play a significant role in the land-based actions of the Boer War.

Six

In a New Century

Following the rebuilding of the dockyard, more than eighty new ships would be built there but, on 29 April 1903, Sheerness launched its last warship, the sloop Cadmus. The Admiralty had decided to switch the yard to a primary function of refitting torpedo boats and their antidote, the torpedo-boat destroyers. The workshops were retooled to deal with these classes of vessel and the two dry docks in the Boat Basin were lengthened during 1906 to allow the largest types of torpedo-boat destroyer to be docked. The dockyard was also given a specialist role constructing torpedo tubes. By the twentieth century the torpedo had become developed as an effective weapon to destroy the ships of an enemy, with the fast torpedo boat as its main means of delivery. Britain had entered into a major building programme for these craft, but so also had the country's bitter new rivals, the Germans. Considerable fears grew at Sheerness that an enemy might mount a surprise night attack, using torpedo boats against the ships in the harbour. In 1903 a protective floating boom was constructed to stretch across the harbour mouth, and powerful searchlights placed along the shoreline to pick out night intruders.

Garrison Point Fort, seen looking across the gun wharf towards its southern flank, still remained the main defence for the dockyard and harbour.

The dockyard facilities as they appeared from the harbour during the early years of the twentieth century.

The battleship *Sans Pareil* at Sheerness protecting both dockyard and harbour as guardship of the port.

View of the *Sans Pareil* from the forecastle looking aft and showing her two powerful $16\frac{1}{2}$ in guns.

Seamen hoisting ammunition aboard a lighter at the dockyard wall.

A large new floating dock, built by Swan & Hunter of Wallsend-on-Tyne for use at Bermuda dockyard, under test in Sheerness harbour on 5 June 1902, the *Sans Pareil* being warped into position for docking.

The *Sans Pareil* brought safely into the dock ready to be shored into position. Water would then be pumped out of the numerous ballast tanks around the dock causing it to rise and lift the ship clear of the sea ready for an inspection of its hull. As soon as the trials had been satisfactorily completed the Bermuda Dock was towed across the Atlantic to its final destination.

A naval parade in Blue Town passing near to the entrance to the pier on the left. The popular Georgian hotel, the Fountain, remained a prominent feature of the old naval quarter.

In Blue Town the dockyard was a dominating presence, its wall extending along the full length of the northern side of the high street.

From 1903 the dockyard employees had a tram service for travelling to and from work. Beyond the two trams, shown passing over the moat bridge at the entrance to Blue Town, can be seen the barrier guard room, the soldiers' recreation block and, on the skyline, the tower of the dockyard church. The trams eventually stopped running in 1917, their role taken over by a bus service.

Dockyard men entering the main gate before fanning out to their various places of work.

The Boat Basin with its covered slipway, standing at the northern end of the yard. In the background, lying outside the boundary of the dockyard, are Garrison Point Fort and Admiralty House.

No.2 Dry Dock, in the Great Basin, was the only dock to be covered. Along with the slip this dock was allocated to the building of new vessels and the covering was to provide protection from the elements while construction progressed.

The sloop *Mutine* in the Great Basin with No.2 Dry Dock behind. In 1912, the cover was removed from the dock when the yard was re-assigned as a refitting facility, with no further building of new ships anticipated.

Work in progress on a destroyer in the Great Basin. The refitting of torpedo boats and destroyers was now the mainstay of the dockyard's workload.

Fitters at work in the dockyard's main fitting shop. There had been major capital expenditure to re-equip the workshops for the new role of the yard as a refit base.

Foundrymen preparing the mould for the casting of a rudder piece in the dockyard foundry.

The Medway floating dock in harbour at Sheerness in 1912. Built by Swan, Hunter & Wigham Richardson at Wallsend-on-Tyne, the new floating dock had arrived in Sheerness harbour on 25 June 1912 to be berthed at special moorings laid for her in Saltpan Reach.

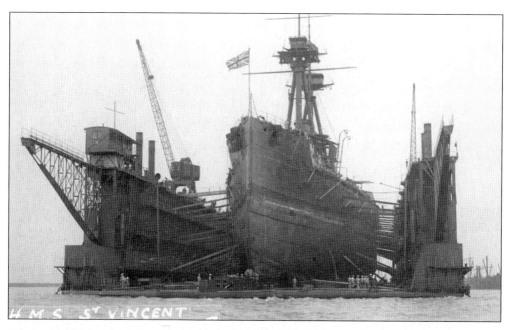

To test the lifting capacity of the Medway floating dock, the battleship *St Vincent* was taken into her on 3 September 1912. Having successfully completed her trials, the floating dock was put into regular service. In 1915 the dock was removed from Sheerness to Jarrow.

In the eastern part of the dockyard, at the far extreme from the noise and bustle of the industrial areas around the basins and workshops, stood the substantial residence of the captain superintendent, the senior officer of the dockyard.

At the rear of the captain superintendent's house were large lawned gardens. A ready supply of naval ratings was always on hand to keep the grass and shrubs in tip-top condition.

On the southern side of the captain superintendent's house was the elegant Dockyard Terrace. The row of houses, provided for the senior dockyard officers, was situated facing a leafy lawned area in one of the few secluded areas of the yard, only the figurehead from the *Devonshire* acting as a reminder of the dockyard location.

Promenading on the town pier was a popular summer pastime for the people of Sheerness who, from the pier end, got a grandstand view of the naval and commercial shipping in the harbour.

Looking inland, those on the pier end were also rewarded with an uninterrupted vista of the adjacent dockyard.

The Sheerness Royal Regatta had, since the mid-nineteenth century, been for many townspeople the highlight of the year. The dockyard's involvement in organising the annual event is to be seen in this Regatta picture, the lighter YC 87 and other yard craft being provided for the judges, stewards and favoured spectators.

On any warm summer's day the families of the dockyard men would head for the beach to enjoy the sun and sea breezes, and to watch the passing ships.

By the second decade of the century the long Edwardian summer was coming to an end and, at Sheerness, there were the first signs of brewing trouble. The directing station was erected on the seafront near to the Catholic church as a sighting tower for powerful searchlights that could pick out hostile ships attempting to attack by night.

Seven

The Great War

After several years of mounting tension war between Britain and Germany finally broke out in August 1914. National fears about enemy spies and saboteurs having already reached almost paranoiac proportions, the security of the dockyard was immediately stepped up, its police force greatly increased and issued with side arms. Throughout the war the dockyard, working at full capacity, would play its part in maintaining the ships of the Royal Navy in a battle-ready condition. As the conflict became quickly stalemated on the Western Front, degenerating into trench warfare, it became suspected that the Germans were going to open up a new offensive by launching a major attack across the North Sea with Sheppey as a likely target. Vast lines of barbed wire entanglements were laid along the seafront at Sheerness, with gun batteries and pill-boxes for machine guns placed at strategic positions ready to repulse the enemy, continuing along the northern coast as far as Shellness at the most easterly point of the island. In 1916 Sheppey was declared to be a restricted military area, effectively one huge army base, and popularly known as Barbed Wire Island. The war ended in 1918, the defences having never been put to the test.

At the beginning of the Great War in 1914 Sheerness was regarded as one of the Royal Navy's key bastions against a possible German attack. It was also a major asset for the Royal Navy as a point of vantage and ready access on the east coast.

From Garrison Point Fort the boom, placed to defend Sheerness Dockyard and the Medway against a possible seaborne attack, stretched across the mouth of the harbour to the distant Martello Tower at the Isle of Grain.

The battle ship *Bulwark* was at rest at its moorings in Sheerness Harbour on 26 November 1914. Suddenly she vanished from sight, disintegrating through a massive internal explosion of her magazines. All her officers and around 750 men perished in an instant. Surprisingly there were fourteen survivors rescued from the water.

Almost exactly six months after the *Bulwark* disaster, another catastrophe would take place in the harbour. As she lay at anchor on 26 May 1915 the minelayer *Princess Irene* was blown to smithereens when her cargo of mines was accidentally detonated. More than 170 of her crew and seventy-six Sheerness Dockyard men who were working onboard were lost. Only a badly burned stoker survived.

Machine gun emplacement in Garrison Point Fort and barbed wire entanglements, viewed from the foreshore midway between Garrison Point and Albemarle Battery.

Between Garrison Point Fort and the foreshore, the west boom machine gun emplacement –
one of the defences to protect the boom – stood behind a wide barrier of barbed wire.

Albemarle Battery and machine gun emplacement, with barbed wire entanglements stretching
along to Garrison Point.

The centre bastion with its three camouflaged towers and machine gun emplacement seen from the sea wall, the protecting spur of the moat lying between it and the foreshore.

Beachfields machine gun emplacement with masses of barbed wire stretching out along the promenade.

The promenade looking towards the navy's directing station. The seafront, which in peacetime would have thronged with strollers, is now strangely deserted except for its military sentinels, with the beach mined and covered in coils of barbed wire.

Even beyond the outskirts of Sheerness at Scrapsgate, the barbed wire and other coastal defences continued to stretch eastwards, vanishing over the distant horizon.

The German U-boat *UC-5* at Sheerness in the summer of 1916. She had become grounded on a shoal in the North Sea on 27 April. When a British destroyer appeared on the scene the submarine was abandoned by her crew. Scuttling charges that had been set failed to detonate and *UC-5* was refloated by the British and carried home.

A group of a dozen of the women employed in the electrical department. The war would cause a social revolution in the dockyard with the first employment of women. A small army of young women in brown overalls appeared to replace the men called away to the armed forces, operating machine tools and performing many other skilled tasks within the various trades of the yard.

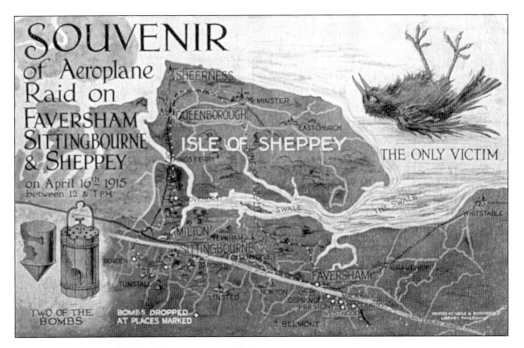

SOUVENIR
of Aeroplane
Raid on
FAVERSHAM
SITTINGBOURNE
& SHEPPEY
on April 16th 1915
between 12 & 1 PM

THE ONLY VICTIM

TWO OF THE
BOMBS

BOMBS DROPPED
AT PLACES MARKED

Above: Throughout the war there was a fear that the dockyard might receive an aerial attack. From time to time an enemy aircraft would fly over the town, and even drop the occasional bomb, but these had little more than nuisance value. A typical incursion is shown on this commemorative postcard, the lone raider veering off to avoid coming within range of the guns at Sheerness.

Left: Matters changed on 5 June 1917 when nineteen Gotha bombers approached the town from the sea. One raider was shot down by the coastal batteries but the others were soon dropping their bombs. Fourteen soldiers and civilians were killed and many more wounded. One of the dead was a worker in the yard and the great Quadranglar Store had a fire which was not put out for three hours, but it was the town that received most damage. The downed aircraft is shown being salvaged after the raid.

The end of the war, the most horrific in terms of loss of human life that the world had ever witnessed, came in November 1918. A gigantic German floating dock arrrived at Sheerness in September 1920, having been towed across the North Sea from Kiel as part of the war reparations.

The German floating dock in harbour at Sheerness. The huge structure was over 700ft long with a breadth of 170ft, and had a lifting weight of 40,000 tons.

Left: With the return to peace, attention was turned in Sheerness to the provision of a war memorial, seen here in the course of erection. The design decided upon was a figure of Liberty standing on a square pedestal base. The names of the dead inscribed on the sides of the pedestal included the civilians killed on the *Princess Irene* and during the air raids on the town.

The War Memorial was formally unveiled by Admiral Sir Hugh Evan-Thomas, commander-in-chief at the Nore, at a service on 29 April 1922. The location of the memorial is clearly shown in this view, standing opposite to the railway station on the road leading to Blue Town, the buildings of the garrison in the background.

Eight

Between the Wars

After the return to peace in 1918 the dockyard work-load plummeted, many men were laid off, and there were persistent rumours of closure. The situation was but slightly alleviated in 1920 when there was an order to build a small seaplane dock. Following this, to keep the yard going at a minimal level, ships launched by private ship builders were ordered to Sheerness for completion. The destroyer Thracian *arrived from Hawthorn Leslie and was completed in 1922, while the submarines L-25 and L-27 from Vickers were completed in 1925 and 1927 respectively. In spite of these measures the Admiralty, continuing to look for economies, announced in 1928 that the yard should close. Fortunately the government, worried about the political fall-out, determined that such action would be premature. In the 1930s the rumblings of new trouble with Germany, now led by Adolf Hitler, caused a modest naval re-armament programme to be enacted which gradually gained pace as German aggression continued. The work situation in the dockyard progressively improved as ships were prepared to be commissioned for sea and, by the time that war broke out in September 1939, the yard would be effectively back to strength.*

The seaplane dock. The last ship to be constructed at Sheerness, she was built in No.1 Dock for the Air Ministry, being floated out on 5 September 1921. She had a lifting capacity of 200 tons and could accommodate two seaplanes at once.

Above: The masting sheers set on the western wall of the Great Basin, a legacy from the days of the sailing navy when the sheers had been a vital piece of equipment for removing and replacing ships' masts. In 1874 the original timber sheers had been replaced by ones of fabricated metal construction.

Left: By 1931 the masting sheers had lost their utility and it was decided that they should be removed. In August dockyard workers began demolition, using acetylene burners to cut almost completely through the bottoms of the front legs of the sheers and then through the rearmost leg of the structure.

Watched from the end of Sheerness Pier by a large crowd that had gathered to witness the event, the sheers suddenly toppled forwards, the front legs snapping off on the impact with the water, which produced a wide column of water nearly 30ft high, and reverberations that shook nearby buildings.

Within seconds the surface of the basin again became smooth as a millpond, with only a small section of one of the broken legs being visible. Riggers afterwards recovered the remains of the sheers from the basin to be taken away as scrap. A prominent dockyard landmark had vanished into history.

HMS *Cornwallis* (seventy-four guns) was an unusual ship being built of teak and launched at Bombay Dockyard in 1813. She had a long and illustrious career: in 1814 she fired the last shots of the Anglo-American wars while, in 1842, the Treaty of Nanking was concluded on her decks, ending the war with China.

By 1865, with her days as a fighting ship over, the *Cornwallis* was about to embark upon the longest if least glamorous phase of her career. In August, having been hulked, she was sunk as a jetty off the dockyard wall at Sheerness. In her new role she was to survive for almost another century, being seen here in a view across her bow at low tide.

The stern and port side of the hulk *Cornwallis* at low water, showing that her teak hull was still in remarkably good condition well over a century after she had been built.

The gun deck of the hulk *Cornwallis* on her port side looking forward, still fundamentally intact despite being awash twice a day at the top of the tides.

The gun deck of the *Cornwallis* on the port side looking aft, the iron rings for securing her guns remaining in place at each side of the gun ports.

To the south, looking sternwards across the deck of the *Cornwallis*, can be seen the end of Sheerness Pier. The corrugated iron building on the left contained two waiting rooms for the officers and men waiting to embark from the jetty.

The view, across the stern of the *Cornwallis* at high tide, towards the victualling store house and former Gunnery School, which had been utilised since February 1937 as a naval training establishment carrying the name HMS Wildfire.

The western range of HMS Wildfire seen from the other side of the entrance to the Small Basin.

The quadrangle of HMS Wildfire still in use as in the days of the Gunnery School for gymnasium, recreation and drill purposes.

The seamen's dining hall in HMS Wildfire. Victualling could be provided for several hundred men.

One of the rooms of HMS Wildfire being used for instructional and recreational purposes.

Six large dormitory rooms were situated in HMS Wildfire for use as sleeping accommodation.

A group photograph showing some of the seamen serving at HMS Wildfire.

Parade of the men of HMS Wildfire. The training establishment closed in 1950, but the building was revitalised in 1954 as an accommodation centre known as the Wildfire Building, in which role it remained until closed down for the final time on 14 October 1959.

Nine
The Final Flourish

Throughout the Second World War Sheerness acted as the base for a large minesweeper flotilla. During the Dunkirk evacuation in 1940 the dockyard became the assembly point for the famed 'little ships' that heroically lifted the army off the French beaches. Four motor launches, each of seventy-three tons, were built in No.4 Dock during the years 1942 and 1943. In spite of its vulnerable east coast situation, the dockyard would remain free of air raids and in 1945 emerged from the war unscathed. The post-war years would be a period of severe retrenchment. There was an increasing under-use of the home dockyards as Britain abandoned its worldwide commitments and the government sought out ways of saving national expenditure. Once again rumours began to circulate locally that the dockyard was to be closed. This time they would prove to be all too true. In February 1958 it was announced in Parliament that the yard was to be closed. Within a year the garrison had been decommissioned and, on 31 March 1960, the closing ceremony took place for the dockyard. A private harbour company then took over both the dockyard and garrison to develop them for commercial use.

An aerial view from the latter years of the dockyard looking out over the Small Basin towards the harbour. Around the basin were clustered some of the most notable of the yard buildings, including Wildfire, the Quadrangular Store, and the large Boat House.

The *Truculent*, T-Class submarine, on 11 January 1950, as she was about to leave the Medway on machinery trials with seventy-nine Royal Navy and dockyard personnel on board. Returning from her trials during the evening of the next day she was struck and sunk off the Nore in a collision with the Swedish tanker SS *Divina*.

The final death toll in the *Truculent* was sixty-four crew and dockyard employees, most of whom had escaped safely to the surface only to die of exposure before rescue arrived. In the picture, the complex operation subsequently mounted to lift the sunken vessel approaches its conclusion.

The *Truculent* was raised on 14 March 1950. She was beached on a spit off Sheerness to be cleared of water and patched, then brought round into the dockyard on 23 March and put into dry dock. In May she was sold to be broken up.

The *Porchester Castle*, one of the navy's Castle Class frigates, at anchor off Sheerness Dockyard in June 1951. During the post-war years, the work of the yard was almost exclusively directed towards the refit of frigates and, more particularly, minesweepers.

M.1783, a motor minesweeper, at her moorings in June 1951 with Garrison Point in the background behind her stern.

The *Kinbrace*, Admiralty salvage vessel (950 tons, two 20mm guns), moored in harbour at Sheerness in September 1952.

The *C.109* coal hulk was long a familiar sight in Sheerness. Starting life in 1865 as the majestic battleship *Agincourt*, she was converted to a coal hulk in 1908 and the following year towed to moorings in Sheerness harbour.

Black and adorned with cranes the *C.109* bore little resemblance to the heavily armed and armoured warship she once was. She remained at Sheerness as a coal hulk for over half a century before being broken up in 1960.

During the late evening of 31 January 1953 the Sheppey sea defences were overwhelmed by the combination of an exceptionally high tide and hurricane force winds, and huge areas of the island were left under water. The breach in the sea wall south of the dockyard is shown. Having survived the buffeting the C.109 coal hulk lies in the background.

Halfway Road, the main route into Sheerness, remained closed for some time. Surrounded by water the town was cut off from the outside world, except by boat, until the rail and road links could be re-established.

Most of the dockyard workers lived in the terraced houses of the back streets of Sheerness. It was obvious that for the immediate future getting to work would be a little problematical.

The *Sirdar*, S-Class Submarine, on her side in No.1 Dry Dock. Water had surged over the 22ft high seawall into the Great Basin and flooded the dockyard causing widespread damage.

The *Berkeley Castle*, a Castle Class corvette, lying on her beam ends in No.2 Dock. She would never again be re-commissioned and arrived to be broken up at Grays in Essex on 29 February 1956.

The Royal Fleet Auxiliary tanker *Wave Prince* (16,480 tons) moored at Sheerness in August 1957. RFA vessels usually had less glamorous careers than their fighting sisters in the RN, but the *Wave Prince* was present at Christmas Island for the H-bomb tests, and acted as escort oiler to the Royal Yacht *Britannia* on several occasions when she went abroad on state visits.

A submarine moored against the south wall of the Great Basin. Behind it, on the left, two vessels obscure the entrance to No.1 Dock.

No.2 Dry Dock, looking westwards towards the dock head from the basin end. Formerly the dockyard's building dock, during its history it had seen many new ships 'floated out'.

The south side of the Small Basin with the Quadrangular Store in the background.

Dockyard lighter YC-83 against the north wall of the Small Basin with the chain testing house and quadrangular storehouse behind.

Another view of the Small Basin looking along its eastern side towards the large Boat House building.

Looking northwards across the Boat Basin's two dry docks and slipway towards Garrison Point.

No.4 Dry Dock looking westwards. One of the two dry docks in the Boat Basin, this was the only dock to be fitted with gates rather than a caisson. The gates were manually operated by capstans.

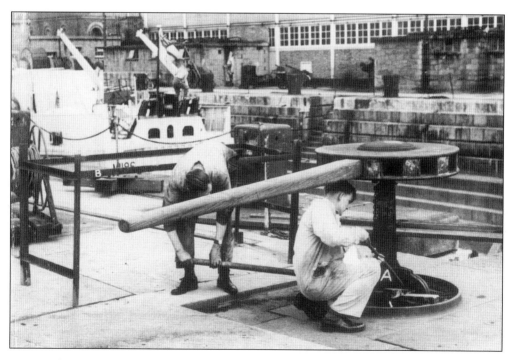

Fitter and mate working on No.4 Dry Dock raising the locking plate on the capstan on the north side of the dock.

Police of the Admiralty Constabulary on duty at the main gate in 1958. In November 1930 the Metropolitan Police's responsibility for the security of the dockyard had been passed to a new force, the Royal Marine Police. Then, in 1949, a newly constituted force, the Admiralty Constabulary, took over.

Within the dockyard looking towards the main gate, the 60ft high Muster Bell Tower and, to its right, the house built in 1830 for the use of the boatswain of the yard.

H. M. DOCKYARD

SHEERNESS

CLOSING CEREMONY

31st March, 1960

Left: Programme for the closing down ceremony of HM Dockyard, Sheerness.

Below: The end of an era. At sunset on 31 March 1960 the Union Jack, flying from the flagstaff at the entrance to the Small Basin, was ceremonially hauled down for the last time and, after almost three centuries, the Royal Dockyard at Sheerness slid into the pages of history.

Ten

A Rich Heritage

As the army and navy prepared to withdraw from Sheerness, and the 2,500-strong workforce braced itself to walk out of the dockyard gates for the last time, they were going to leave behind an important part of the nation's architectural heritage. Among a rich and varied collection of Georgian structures were the basins, dry docks and slipway, and the industrial, administration and residential buildings of the dockyard. In addition there were some very fine early Victorian structures including a unique boat house and the fort at Garrison Point. Also at the dockyard, and older than any of its buildings, there remained the venerable old hulk Cornwallis, *a survivor from the time of the Napoleonic wars. The Admiralty was aware of the special significance of much that it was abandoning, and the need for its continued protection. In May 1959 the First Lord of the Admiralty announced in Parliament that twenty-five residences and other buildings, including the Quadrangular Store and Admiralty House, had been listed under the Town and Country Planning Act of 1947 as buildings of important architectural and historical interest. This would be the final act by the Admiralty to secure the future of the buildings before relinquishing its responsibility for them.*

Looking out to sea at sunset through the entrance of the Small Basin with its swing bridge; the Wildfire Building is on the left.

Central offices facing the Wildfire Building across the entrance to the Small Basin. The central offices and Wildfire Building, originally the officers' offices and victualling storehouse, were two of the first completed buildings of Rennie's new dockyard.

The great Quadrangular Store seen looking across the Small Basin in an easterly direction from the Wildfire Building.

The Quadrangular Store was commenced in 1824 to the designs of architect Edward Holl, Surveyor of Buildings to the Admiralty, and completed in 1829. The massive five-storey building occupied a 3.1 acre site.

The iron gates and doors of the Quadrangular Store. The big rusticated granite archways were said to resemble the entrance to the old Newgate Prison.

Part of the vast storage areas available in the Quadrangular Store. Within the building was housed in vast array the immense variety of stores and equipment that were required for the running of the Royal Navy.

An aerial view of the large Boat House. At 210ft long and 135ft wide, it was commenced in 1858 to the plans of Godfrey T. Greene, Admiralty Director of Works, and completed in 1860.

The Boat House viewed from the south. The structure was of international importance in the history of architecture, being the world's earliest multi-storey iron-framed building, and a precursor to all the world's later skyscrapers.

Internally the Boat House had, to each side of a central aisle, three floor levels for the storage of ships' boats. Each ascending level had slightly less head clearance and the smallest boats were kept on the top floor.

Above: The chain testing house. It was brick built in 1856 and, although a functional building, given vigorously modelled windows, which were round-headed below and circular above, and set in recessed panels of the same shape.

Left: The inside of the chain testing house showing the machinery used in order to proof-test chains for strength before they were put into service.

Above: The ship fitting shop, situated behind the slipway in the most northerly part of the dockyard, was one of the newer buildings, being erected in the 1870s.

Right: The smithery. The hard labour of the forging operations was reduced in April of 1846 through the introduction of two steam-powered drop hammers, of 50cwt and 10cwt respectively, the larger with a fall of 4ft capable of delivering up to 40 blows per minute at a maximum impact force of eighteen tons.

The chimney of one of the large furnaces for the forges within the smithery.

Smithery No.2, built in 1856 to the plans of Godfrey T. Greene, could be regarded as the prototype for his 1859 Boat House masterpiece with which it shared significant design features.

Above: An unobscured corner of the working mast house, one of the earliest buildings in the dockyard which, reflecting the changing nature of ship construction, had later become the shipwrights' machine shop.

Right: Electricity had first been introduced on board Royal Navy ships in 1876, following which there had been a steady growth in its utilization. Reflecting this, in the early years of the twentieth century the electrical fitting shop was established within the former mast and top shed as shown.

Left: A survivor of the days of wooden ship construction, this building was one of the original suppling kilns built in 1828. Within, planks for ships' timbers were boiled in sea water which allowed them to be shaped to suit the curving profiles of the bow and stern quarters. The building found a final use as a chargeman's cabin.

Below: No.1 Dry Dock looking from the east. In the years following the Second World War this dock became dedicated almost exclusively to submarine dockings.

The two-storey Archway Block. Originally built in 1830 to the design of Edward Holl as mould lofts and saw pits with joiners' shops etc. above.

Through the arch of Archway Block lay the road passing eastwards along the main axis of the dockyard.

At its far end the road passed between the captain superintendent's house and the end of Dockyard Terrace (off on the right) to terminate at the dockyard wall. Set in the wall was the private entrance that gave the captain access to the dockyard church and outside world.

The rear of the captain superintendent's house, a spacious mansion built in 1830 to the plans of Admiralty architect George L. Taylor.

The Naval Terrace (1830) and church (1828), erected outside the dockyard wall at the eastern end of the yard, were also the work of George L. Taylor.

The interior of the dockyard church looking eastwards. The church was gutted by an accidental fire in 1881 and had to undergo a major refurbishment.

Above: Admiralty House, built in 1827 in the Greek revival style, was the most prestigious naval residence in Sheerness.

Left: Admiralty House's monumental entrance hall in which steps and a screen of two Ionic columns greeted visitors. Beyond, the main stairway gave access to the landing and two state rooms above. The elegant scene has been slightly marred by the later addition of functional dockyard-style heating.

Eleven
Postscript

As the newly constituted Harbour Company assumed control of the former dockyard and adjacent garrison at Sheerness in 1960, placed in its care was the stewardship of a large number of historic buildings, twenty-five of them scheduled as being of particular architectural distinction. For a century and more the naval and military authorities had ensured that the buildings and installations had been maintained in first-class condition. It would now fall to the new ownership to demonstrate the same sense of responsibility that its predecessors had shown towards the buildings, and to continue to carefully oversee their preservation. In developing the buildings for commercial purposes it would require care and imagination to ensure that they would be sympathetically adapted to the new uses to which they were to be put, with as much of their original character as possible being retained. Also needed would be the instigation of an effective programme of running repairs to keep the buildings in a condition that was both worthy of their special status, and necessary to secure their continued existence for future generations as part of the nation's great maritime heritage.

THE SHEERNESS HARBOUR ESTATE

The former dockyard and garrison in the early years after closure. In the foreground the moat and the army playing fields in Well Marsh can be clearly seen.

In 1957 the Admiralty had finally ordered that the *Cornwallis* should be removed, but the task proved more difficult than anticipated and, when it was known that the dockyard was going to close, the project was cancelled, leaving her with her upper decks ripped off as shown.

The *Cornwallis* was inherited by the new owners of the dockyard in 1960. Preservation would not be a consideration and demolition was ordered. She was burned to the waterline and the submerged part of the hull was refloated, beached south of the dockyard, and broken up.

The historic Admiralty House in 1958. The building had been official residence of the commander-in-chief at the Nore until 1907, with subsequent roles that included residence of the commander-in-chief's Home Fleet, and it has seen many distinguished occupants.

Admiralty House under demolition in January 1964. Today the deserted terminus building of a failed shipping company stands on the site.

Left: An aerial view looking eastwards across Garrison Point, beyond which Admiralty House and every building of the former garrison have been erased from the scene.

Below: Garrison Point Fort from the sea. A Grade II listed building, the Victorian armoured plating was taken from its gun embrasures in 1968 and sold for scrap.

Within Garrison Point Fort the handsome cast-iron verandas, installed during the fort's construction, are left to rot and decay.

The three tall towers of the Centre Battery, a familiar Sheerness landmark, though long derelict and neglected, still survive.

Following the closure of the dockyard in 1960, the main gate of 1821, with its Georgian colonaded entrance, did not survive demolition for long.

The site of the main gate at what is still the main entrance to the former dockyard.

Above: The massive Quadranglar Store, part of the nation's heritage as a unique gem of Georgian industrial architecture, had its demolition authorised in 1977 and was pulled down in the following year.

Right: Not all of the Quadrangular Store was destroyed. Today its little wooden clock tower stands on the ground in solitary isolation as a memorial to the lost architectural classic.

The historic Great Basin, which was protected by a Grade II listed status, was buried under thousands of tons of infill during 1977. The Small Basin had already received identical treatment.

The Great Basin's three Grade II listed dry docks at the same time suffered a similar fate; here the infilling of No.1 Dock nears completion.

Construction in hand for a large steelworks on the former army playing fields at Well Marsh in September 1971.

The completed steelworks brought needed employment to Sheerness, but it was also an extensive industrial complex on the fringe of the town that would lead to unwelcome pollution problems.

The Boat House, a building of internationally recognised importance for its innovative construction, and protected by a Grade I listing, still survives at the moment.

The interior of the famous Boat House, the boats now gone. Since being placed in private hands, years of neglect have left the building in need of a major overhaul.

The former Dockyard College, once provider of technical education for generations of apprentices, now finds use as office accommodation.

A small oasis of still standing ex-dockyard buildings. From right to left: the former Dockyard College Engineering Laboratory, two-storey Expense Accounts Office and Saw Mills. The buildings beyond are modern sheds on the sites of the demolished smitheries, boiler shop and stores.

Ships now regularly use the port facilities of the former dockyard, disgourging thousands of imported cars and vans.

A sea of imported vehicles awaiting transportation to dealerships across Britain. They stand in a massive parking area to the south of the former dockyard that, at over three times the dockyard's area, was illegally built on reclaimed mud flats.

The Archway Block, now called Archway House, today houses the port offices.

The former captain superintendent's house, a Grade II listed building, now unoccupied and in increasing need of attention.

In the north-eastern corner of the large gardens of the captain superintendent's house stood the stable block for his horses. After dockyard closure the stables were for a time used as a stevedores' club. Behind them can be seen the rear of the house originally built for the boatswain of the yard.

Naval Terrace. The eight substantial houses constructed to house the senior naval officers of the dockyard, have now been sold off to private owners.

Dockyard Terrace, a row of five Grade II listed buildings. Since being given the aggrandizing (but anachronistic) name of Regency Close, it is currently converted into tenancies and is in a faded and deteriorating condition.

To the rear of Dockyard Terrace, with the large gardens now swept away to create a large parking area used as additional storage space for imported vehicles.

For a while used as a youth centre, the dockyard church was then for many years left boarded up and empty.

The dockyard church, a protected Grade II listed building and long-term white elephant, was gutted by a fire which began during the early hours of 31 May 2001. Its fate is now uncertain, perhaps to join more than fifty substantial Georgian or early Victorian buildings that have now vanished from the former dockyard and garrison.